D1511280

The Pros and Cons of
BIOMASS POWER
Isabel Thomas

rosen publishing's
rosen
central
New York

Published in 2008 by The Rosen Publishing Group, Inc.
29 East 21st Street, New York, NY 10010

First Edition

Series Editor: Jennifer Schofield
Editor: Debbie Foy
Consultant: Rob Bowden
Designer: Jane Hawkins
Cover designer: Paul Cherrill
Picture Researcher: Diana Morris
Illustrator: Ian Thompson
Indexer: Sue Lightfoot

Picture Acknowledgments:
Ken Ayres/Ecoscene: 1, 20. Andy Binns/Ecoscene: 10. Eddi Boehnke/
Zefa/Corbis: front cover. Joerg Boethling/Still Pictures: 30. Rob Bowden/
EASI-Images; 8 14, 45. Joel Creed/Ecoscene: 13. Courtesy of DC Media
Services: 40. Mark Edwards/Still Pictures: 27. Chris Fairclough/EASI-Images/
CFW Images: 43. Pat Groves/Ecoscene: 17. Roy Maconachie/EASI-Images: 28.
Ed Parker/EASI-Images: 5, 18. Louie Psihoyos/Corbis: 22. Reuters/Corbis; 40.
Jorgen Schytte/Still Pictures: 32. Skyscan/SPL: 40. Keren Su/Photolibrary: 35.
Robert Walker/Ecoscene: front cover br.

Library of Congress Cataloging-in-Publication Data

Thomas, Isabel, 1980-
  the pros and cons of Biomass / Isabel Thomas.
     p. cm. -- (The energy debate)
  Includes index.
  ISBN-13: 978-1-4042-3742-1 (library binding)
  ISBN-10: 1-4042-3742-9 (library binding)
  1. Biomass energy--Juvenile literature. 2. Biomass energy--Economic aspects--Juvenile literature. I. Title.
  TP360.T4855 2007
  333.95'39--dc22
                              2006039139

Manufactured in China

Contents

CHAPTER 1 | Biomass power and the energy debate

Energy makes all life on Earth possible. Energy from food allows plants and animals to live and grow. Heat energy cooks food and warms homes. Light energy and sound energy allow us to see and hear. All these forms of energy share the ability to do work—to make something happen.

Energy cannot be made or destroyed, but it can be changed from one form to another. The energy industry makes billions of dollars converting energy into useful forms, such as electricity, and supplying it around the world.

In demand

Most of the energy used to generate electricity comes from burning coal, oil, and natural gas. These fossil fuels were created over millions of years from the remains of dead animals and plants. Transportation also consumes huge amounts of fossil fuels. Approximately 2,000 million gallons (7,500 million liters) of oil are converted into gasoline and diesel every day. This would fill almost 4,000 Olympic-sized swimming pools.

An energy crisis?

Fossil fuels are running out. Coal reserves may last for up to 300 years, but the production of oil and gas is expected to slow down during the middle of this century. As coal reserves become harder to find, supplies will quickly become too expensive to use. The burning of fossil fuels is also creating serious environmental problems. Fumes emitted by vehicles and industry result in hundreds of thousands of deaths every year. On a global level, fossil fuel emissions are warming the atmosphere and threaten to cause long-term climate change.

> **"** If we don't have a proactive energy policy, we'll just wind up using [dirtier fossil fuels], and... eventually our civilization will collapse. But it doesn't have to end that way. We have a choice. **"**
>
> Martin Hoffert, Professor of Physics, New York University

Global warming

Certain gases in the atmosphere act like the glass walls of a greenhouse. They trap some of the Sun's heat and stop it from escaping back into space. These "greenhouse gases" keep the

Earth warm enough to make life possible. Carbon dioxide (CO_2) is one of the most abundant greenhouse gases.

Burning fossil fuels—coal, oil, and natural gas—releases extra CO_2 that is increasing the natural "greenhouse effect." This process is causing the Earth's atmosphere to warm up, and could lead to a rise in sea levels, severe flooding, and the spread of diseases, violent weather, drought, extinction of many species, and food shortages.

▽ Oil powers most of the world's 800 million vehicles. World oil use grew by 50 million gallons (190 million liters) per day in 2005.

However, every source of energy has its downsides. Renewable energy resources (such as wood, crops, solar power, and water power) are not as convenient and accessible as fossil fuels. This makes them more expensive to use. Renewable energies also bring their own environmental problems, such as their impact on the landscape. No single alternative energy source has the potential to meet all of the world's future energy needs alone. Therefore, the challenge we face is to build a global energy mix that will tackle the problems of climate change, and will supply a source of reliable and affordable energy into the future.

Biomass then and now

Scientists have experimented with alternative sources of energy for centuries, but serious interest in renewable energy sources began in the 1970s, when the price of oil rose steeply. This shocked countries that were used to buying cheap energy. They rushed to find ways to reduce their dependency on imported oil.

When the price of oil fell again in the 1980s, enthusiasm for renewable energies faded. However, evidence for global warming continued to grow.

In 1997, the Kyoto agreement was drawn up to commit more economically developed countries (MEDCs) to reducing greenhouse gas emissions. These countries agreed to significantly reduce carbon emissions by 2012. In the early 2000s, Kyoto targets, high oil prices, and fears about energy security have led to renewed investment in renewable energies—including biomass.

▽ Biomass is currently the world's most common "alternative" energy resource. However, much of this use is unsustainable and is contributing to global warming.

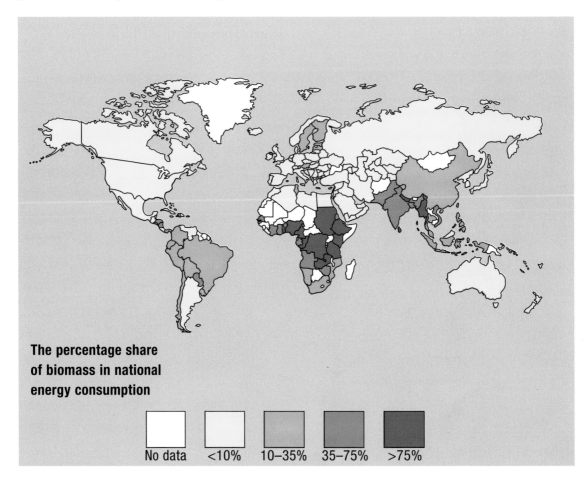

The percentage share of biomass in national energy consumption

No data   <10%   10–35%   35–75%   >75%

A simple source of energy

Biomass fuel is any material from living things that can be used as an energy source. When wood, plants, and animal droppings are burned, the chemical energy stored in them is released as heat and light. Biomass is the oldest energy source in the world. There is evidence that human beings were burning wood 400,000 years ago, and it is still the main form of energy used by 2 billion people in less economically developed countries (LEDCs). In Ethiopia, for example, traditional fuels provide 95 percent of all energy.

Scientists are finding new ways to use biomass energy. It can be burned to produce steam for making electricity or to heat buildings. It can also be converted into more concentrated energy sources, such as liquid fuel or gas. The commercial use of biomass is growing, but MEDCs generate just 3 percent of their energy using biomass.

Carbon neutral

When plants grow, they absorb CO_2 from the air, storing the carbon in their leaves and stems. When a plant is burned, the stored carbon is then released back into the atmosphere. If every plant that is burned is replaced, then in theory, burning biomass does not increase the amount of CO_2 in the atmosphere.

Biomass fuels are, therefore, described as carbon neutral. However, most biomass use around the world is currently unsustainable. Forests and crops are not replanted, or more energy is used in harvesting and processing the biomass than it produces. This contributes to global warming and local air pollution.

The International Energy Agency (IEA) predicts that global energy demand will increase by 50 to 60 percent from 2004 to 2030, as populations grow and the standard of living in many parts of the world rises. If this energy is generated from fossil fuels, then it is likely that greenhouse gas emissions will rise by 50 per cent. To avoid an energy crisis, we will need to find alternative energy sources. The IEA estimates that biomass energy could meet more than a third of the world's current energy needs—but only if it can be developed into an affordable and clean energy resource.

> " Biomass is potentially the world's largest sustainable energy source. "
>
> Yoshihiro Hatano, manager, World Energy Council

CHAPTER 2 — What Is biomass energy?

All of the energy we use can be traced back to the Sun, the Earth's nearest star. Inside the Sun, hydrogen atoms fuse to create helium, releasing vast amounts of energy. This travels through space in the form of electromagnetic radiation—including light rays and infrared (heat) waves. A tiny fraction reaches the Earth.

When the infrared radiation hits the Earth's surface, it heats the surrounding air, water, and ground.

▽ Millions of families in the LEDCs of the world rely on simple biomass-burning stoves for cooking and heating.

This keeps the planet warm enough to support life. Heat from the Sun also drives weather patterns and the water cycle, which are the sources of wind power and water power.

Nature's power plants

Light energy from the Sun is essential for life on Earth. Green plants absorb sunlight and convert it into chemical energy by a complex process called *photosynthesis*. This energy is passed on to animals when they eat plants or other animals. When plants, animals, and their wastes (biomass) are burned, the stored chemical energy is released as heat and light.

Biomass can be seen as a way of storing solar energy. During the process of photosynthesis, CO_2 from the air, and water from the ground, are converted into complex substances that store a great deal of energy in their chemical bonds, including sugars, cellulose, carbohydrates, proteins, and oils. Growing plants store carbon, so using biomass energy is a way of recycling the carbon over and over again—as long as the harvested biomass is replanted. Compared with the burning of fossil fuels, this potentially reduces the level of carbon emissions that stay in the atmosphere.

Low efficiency

Plants can capture only a certain part of sunlight. Even the most efficient plants convert just 6.7 percent of the Sun's energy into stored chemical energy. However, plants grow in large quantities over very wide areas of land, and they store up the chemical energy, even when the Sun is not shining. This gives biomass great potential as a future source of energy.

Before the Industrial Revolution, almost all human energy needs were met by burning biomass, such as wood. Since 1850, most of the world's energy has been supplied by coal, oil, and natural gas. These fossil fuels are formed from plants and animals that decayed millions of years ago.

They are much more concentrated stores of chemical energy than living plants. However, coal, gas, and oil reserves are being used up 100,000 times faster than they are formed. The carbon absorbed millions of years ago cannot all be reabsorbed by growing plants, and unlike biomass, fossil fuels cannot be renewed.

THE ARGUMENT: Biomass fuels are a better source of energy than fossil fuels

For:
- Biomass can be replanted to absorb the carbon released when it is burned.
- Biomass is sustainable—it will never run out.
- Biomass can be grown in almost every country of the world.

Against:
- Fossil fuels are more concentrated stores of energy.
- Fossil fuels are currently cheaper than biomass fuels.
- Plants require a lot of land to grow.
- Fossil fuels come "fully made."

The easiest way to release energy from biomass is by burning it directly.
In many LEDCs, firewood is the most important source of energy for both heating and cooking. In MEDCs, fossil fuels are used mainly for everyday needs, but many people use wood for log fires and charcoal on barbecues.

CASE STUDY:
Biomass stoves

Biomass is still a major source of energy in the rural areas of LEDCs. Traditional fuels, such as wood, animal dung, and crop residues, are often burned directly on open fires or simple ovens made from local materials. Yak dung is a major fuel among Tibetan herdsmen, who live far from power lines and distribution networks for fuels such as coal. Before the dung is burned, it is sun-dried into flat cakes. When it is dried, it can be easily stacked and stored, and burns when lit. In the frozen Tibetan mountains, dung-

△ Herbivore droppings, such as this yak dung, can be dried in the Sun, pressed into flat cakes and burnt as a useful source of biomass fuel.

burning stoves are an important source of heat for cooking, boiling water, and warming rooms. The fuel is also free, and is relatively easy to collect compared to wood or shrubs in the barren Tibetan landscape. One disadvantage of burning dung is that it produces a lot of soot and smoke, which can cause eye and lung diseases.

Biomass can also be used to generate electricity. The heat is used to boil water and make steam, which drives turbines under high pressures and temperatures. This requires large quantities of biomass fuel—of which there are three main sources: agricultural waste, energy crops, and domestic and industrial waste.

Agricultural waste

Around 30 percent of the world's agricultural land is devoted to growing crops for food, clothing, animal feed, construction, and luxury items, such as tea and coffee. Only a small part of most crops is used to make the finished product; the rest of the crop goes to waste, but it could be used for energy production. In LEDCs around the world, many types of agricultural waste, including animal manure (or digested plant matter), are burned for cooking and heating.

Energy crops

Some crops are grown for the sole purpose of energy production. These "energy crops" include grasses (such as sugar cane), grains (such as wheat), and trees (such as eucalyptus). Trees suitable for energy crops grow very fast and resprout after being cut close to the ground. Poplar, maple, and willow trees are best for cooler areas, sycamore for temperate climates, and eucalyptus for tropical climates.

Perennial grasses, such as sugar cane and switch grass, last for more than two growing seasons, so they can also be harvested without replanting.

Plant material will burn well only if it is dry. Good energy crops produce a high yield of dry material per acre, so less land is needed to produce a certain amount of energy. An energy crop should also produce more energy than is used to grow and process it. When farming methods involve the use of heavy machinery, chemicals, such as pesticides and fertilizers, and transportation, there is a danger that more energy may be used up in the production of the energy crop than is released when the crop is burned.

Domestic and industrial waste

Domestic households and industry produce billions of tons of rubbish every year. Many countries have begun to recycle materials such as plastics, paper, metals, and glass, but organic waste, such as rotting food and garden refuse, ends up in landfill sites where it gives off methane (or "landfill gas"). Methane is another type of greenhouse gas that is associated with climate change. Some countries, such as the United States, Australia, France, and Denmark, have begun to burn rubbish, or the methane gas it releases, as a source of biomass energy.

From biomass to fuel

Almost all types of biomass can be converted into liquid, solid, or gas fuels. These fuels are a more concentrated source of energy than dry biomass; they are easier to transport and can be used to power everything from vehicles and boilers, to electricity generators. Fuels derived from biomass are produced through different biological, chemical, and thermal (heating) processes.

Biological processes

Starchy plants, such as sugar beet, corn, sugar cane, and potatoes, can be fermented to produce liquid fuels. Carbohydrates (such as starch) are long strings of sugar molecules. Yeast and bacteria produce enzymes that break down a plant's sugars and starches to make a type of alcohol called *ethanol*. Ethanol is filtered to remove impurities and is then distilled.

Ethanol produced by fermenting corn or sugar cane has been used in vehicle engines for many years. In Brazil and the United States, large quantities of ethanol are blended with gasoline to use in car engines. This adds oxygen to the engine's combustion process, allowing the gasoline to burn more efficiently, so less is used. When biomass is left to rot, microbes break it down to produce a mix of methane and CO_2. Sewage, animal droppings, or industrial waste can be collected in special digesters to capture these gases. The biogas can be burned for cooking, heating, and generating electricity.

Chemical processes

Biodiesel is a fuel made from plant oils rather than carbohydrates. Plants, such as rapeseed and soybean, are pressed to squeeze out oils known as *triglycerides*. These are heated to purify the oil, and alcohol (methanol or ethanol) and a catalyst are added to break the triglycerides down into fuel that can be used in diesel engines.

Agricultural waste is known as *cellulosic biomass*. Cellulose is a carbohydrate, but unlike starch, it is difficult to break down into sugars for fermenting. Around 990 million tons of cellulosic waste is produced in the United States every year. Energy researchers are currently exploring ways of breaking it down using biological and chemical processes.

" Cellulosic biofuels are at least as likely as hydrogen to be a future, sustainable transportation fuel of choice. "

Yerina Mugica, Research Associate, U.S. Natural Resources Defense Council

At the moment, this is too expensive to use commercially, but the U.S. Natural Resources Defense Council (NRDC) hopes that fuels derived from cellulosic biomass could supply up to 30 percent of U.S. fuel needs by 2050.

Thermal processes

Wood and other types of biomass that contain woody fibers (such as crop waste and peanut kernels) can be heated to produce solid, liquid, and gas fuels. A process called *pyrolysis* produces charcoal. During pyrolysis, wood is heated in the absence of air (so that it does not burn), and it breaks down into a mix of liquids,

△ Ethanol derived from sugar cane is a popular vehicle fuel in Brazil. It is blended with gasoline and sold in regular gas stations.

gases, and a solid called *char* (or solid carbon). All of these products can be used as fuel. Charcoal is an important source of energy in many African, Latin American, and Asian countries. It is lighter than wood, and burns more slowly, so it is a popular fuel in towns and cities. More advanced thermal technology is being developed, including the process of gasification (see page 17), where high temperatures are used to convert cellulosic biomass directly into a form of gas fuel.

CHAPTER 3 — Biomass in practice

Most biomass power is currently used on a small scale. The most popular forms include wood burning heaters and biogas digesters. Wood is used as a fuel in many households in Europe, especially in rural areas of Sweden, France, and Austria. Biomass-fired heating and electricity generating plants have also been established worldwide near industries that produce wood waste, such as paper mills and timber yards.

▽ Simple biogas digesters allow families in LEDCs to generate a useful fuel from animal and crop waste matter.

Biogas digesters

Biomass that is too wet to be burned directly can be converted to biogas in a digester. Animal dung, crop waste, sewage sludge, and household waste can all be treated in this way. A typical digester is a large insulated tank or pit covered with a dome to collect the gas, which is released through an outlet pipe. Biogas digestion is one of the cheapest and easiest ways for small communities to obtain useful energy.

Over 2.5 million biogas digesters are used in India. Dung from cattle owned by a family is fed into the digester.

> **"** [With a biomass boiler] we can produce our own fuel on site, be almost carbon neutral and heat our own buildings. **"**
>
> Sam Whatmore, Forestry professional, and member of South West Wood Fuels, a fuelwood supply cooperative, U.K.

As a result of the warm conditions, bacteria break down the plant material present in the dung and convert it to methane gas (about 65 per cent) and CO_2 (about 35 per cent).

The biogas is burned to release energy for cooking, lighting, refrigeration, heating, and running machinery. This reduces the number of trees that need to be cut down for firewood. It also converts methane, a potent greenhouse gas, into the less potent CO_2. The leftover sludge from the digester is rich in nutrients and can be used as fertilizer.

Some farmers in MEDCs are starting to use biogas digesters. A digester that can process the dung from 500 cows costs around $280,000. The biogas can be burned to heat the digester (which must be kept at 95°F or 35°C) and farm buildings, or to produce electricity on a small scale.

CASE STUDY:
Power from waste wood

Every year, almost 900 million trees are cut down to provide raw materials for U.S. paper and pulp mills. Weyerhaeuser, a forestry products company, is planning to use waste from its paper and pulp business as a source of energy, reducing its greenhouse gas emissions by 40 percent by 2020. This will be equivalent to the greenhouse gases produced by 700,000 vehicles in a year. The company burns wood waste in boilers that generate steam and electrical energy to power the paper mills. The mills already get 72 percent of their energy from biomass, and this is set to increase. All the forests used to supply the mills are sustainable, since new trees are planted to replace those felled, so the energy will be carbon neutral. The company itself will save money on fossil fuels, and guard against energy price rises in the future.

Generating electricity from biomass

Biomass fuels, such as wood, wood waste, and household waste, can all be used for electricity generation.

Willow and poplar are efficient energy crops that can be coppiced when they are a year old, so that a lot of stems grow quickly. Wood can be harvested every three years without the need to replant the trees. The first harvest takes four years, so early planning and investment is needed. Steam escapes when fresh wood burns, reducing the heat given out, so harvested wood must be dried before it is used.

Wood waste is a cheaper and more immediate source of biomass. Wood that has been used in households or offices, or as railroad sleepers, is usually very dry, so it produces a lot of heat when it is burned. However, it has often been treated with chemicals, such as paints, oil, glue, and varnish, which give off polluting emissions.

Cofiring: using biomass to supplement fossil fuels

Building new power stations to burn biomass uses a large amount of energy. It is better to adapt existing power stations to burn biomass alongside coal, gas, or oil. Coal is the most polluting of the fossil fuels and is used for almost 40 percent of the world's electricity production, so cofiring with just 5 percent biomass fuel could significantly reduce carbon emissions on a global scale.

Biomass can be blended with the coal directly, but this can cause problems. Bulky, soft plant material is not as easy to handle as brittle coal. It is more efficient to turn the biomass into gas and pump it into the coal boiler. This process is called *gasification*.

THE ARGUMENT: Waste wood should be used as biomass fuel

For:
- It reduces sulphur dioxide and nitrous oxide emissions.
- Money is made from a waste product.
- It is renewable if wood is taken from sustainable plantations.
- No net CO_2 emissions if wood is taken from sustainable plantations.

Against:
- Treated wood waste has chemicals applied to it.
- Wood is bulky and contains two-thirds less energy than fossil fuels per ton.
- Gives waste wood a value, so does not encourage efficient use of forests.

CASE STUDY:
Cofueling Drax

Drax, in Yorkshire, England, is Europe's biggest power station. At full capacity, it burns 12 million tons of coal a year. In order to meet government targets for lowering carbon dioxide emissions, Drax began to develop the technology for cofiring with biomass fuels. Around 200,000 tons of dry biomass was added to its furnaces in 2005, lowering the CO_2 emissions from the power station by around 495,000 tons. However, in 2006, Drax cut the amount of biomass fuel it was

△ Drax has developed new technology to burn biomass and coal together more efficiently.

burning by 90 per cent. It became more profitable to meet emissions targets by buying "carbon credits" instead. Under this scheme, companies such as Drax can increase their emissions allowance by buying "spare" carbon allowances from other companies. The overall emissions allowance remains the same, but environmental groups are unhappy that Drax is not doing more to reduce this figure.

Biomass gasification
A gasifier uses high temperatures to break down solid biomass into a mix of methane, hydrogen, and carbon monoxide gases. This gas passes through a scrubber to remove small particles of soot. It burns more cleanly and efficiently than the solid biomass from which it was made.

Tars, water vapor, solid char, and ash are also produced. In a second reactor, the char can be burned to provide heat for the first step. Unlike solid biomass, which burns only when it is dry, a huge range of biomass can be gasified. This includes wood, charcoal, crop residues, energy crops, and organic wastes, such as sewage sludge.

Generating fuel from biomass

Oil converted into gasoline and diesel and used in vehicles is responsible for a quarter of global greenhouse gas emissions. The problem is becoming worse as 65 million cars are added to the world's roads every year. As oil prices and the demand for cleaner fuel rises, liquid fuels made from biomass are attracting great interest.

The ethanol industry

Ethanol is the world's most widely used biofuel, with 9.6 billion gallons (36.5 billion liters) produced in 2005. It shares some important properties with gas. It is just as easy to transport, store, and transfer to cars. The energy content is similar, so cars powered on ethanol can drive just as fast and just as far. Another advantage is that it can be easily blended with gasoline to use in existing engines. Heavy vehicles, such as trucks and buses, traditionally run on diesel, but tests of an ethanol-diesel mix in buses in Stockholm, Sweden, show that large vehicles can use cheaper ethanol, too.

Brazil is the world's biggest ethanol producer, producing over 4 billion gallons (16 billion liters) a year from sugar cane. All gasoline sold in Brazil must contain at least 20 percent ethanol, powering the equivalent of 4 million cars.

▽ Only a small part of every sugar cane crop is used to make sugar. The waste can be converted into bioethanol to fuel vehicles.

The United States is the second biggest ethanol producer, producing 2.6 billion gallons (10 billion liters) per year. This is only 2 percent of the total gas used in the U.S., but production is growing every year. In the U.K., the Tesco supermarket chain includes 5 percent ethanol in its filling stations in parts of the country. Adding 5 percent ethanol to all U.K. gasoline would reduce carbon emissions equivalent to taking 1 million cars off the road.

Corn ethanol

In the U.S., research into biomass energy sources has focused on the production of ethanol from corn. Of the 900 million gallons (3,400 million liters) of ethanol currently used in California, only 5 percent is produced in the state. California is aiming to produce 20 percent of its own biofuels by 2010 and 40 percent by 2020. A large grain milling company here will open eight ethanol plants by 2008, which will produce a total of 420 million gallons (1,600 million liters) of ethanol per year. Car companies are racing to design and sell "flex fuel" vehicles that can run on any blend of ethanol and gasoline.

By-products of ethanol

The process used to make ethanol has several useful by-products, including animal feed, corn syrup, cornmeal, corn oil, and CO_2, which can be collected to make carbonated drinks. Ethanol can be used to make other chemicals currently derived from oil.

THE ARGUMENT: Ethanol is a good fuel

For:

- It releases less carbon monoxide, nitrogen oxide, and sulphur (pollutants that cause health problems in cities) than gasoline.
- It can be distributed within the current infrastructure.
- It can be blended with gasoline to use in existing engines.
- It contains no lead additives.
- It reduces smog.
- Ethanol spills biodegrade faster than oil spills.
- Other useful chemicals are produced when it is made.
- Production costs are decreasing.

Against:

- Potential to reduce costs of production is low.
- Ethanol does not burn as easily as gas in cold weather, so vehicles would need to warm it first.
- Emissions of reactive chemicals, called aldehydes, are greater than gasoline, and it is hard to predict their long-term effect.

Using vegetable oils

Vegetable oils pressed from sunflower seeds, soybeans, palm oil, rapeseed, and other oily plants can be used directly as a fuel for certain types of heating systems. Vegetable oils can also be used as fuel in diesel engines.

Biodiesel

For commercial use, vegetable oils are treated with alcohol to turn them into a more efficient fuel called *biodiesel*. In European countries, such as Austria, Italy, and France, biodiesel made from rapeseed is more widely used than ethanol. In Germany, where almost 40 percent of cars are diesel-powered, more than 1,800 filling stations sell 530 million gallons (2,000 million liters) of biodiesel a year. However, this is still just 3 percent of Germany's total diesel consumption.

△ Oily plants such as this field of yellow rapeseed can be crushed to extract their natural oils, which are used to make biodiesel.

Although European countries have been the world's main biodiesel producers for years, other countries around the world, including Canada, India, and Brazil, are developing a biodiesel industry. In the United States, soybeans are the most widely grown biodiesel crop. The first biodiesel pump in the U.S. opened in 2001, and today there are over 600 outlets.

Most of the world's buses, boats, and trucks are diesel-powered. Biodiesel is a good substitute, because it halves air pollution and cuts cancer-causing substances by 94 per cent. In the U.S., school buses are starting to run on biodiesel, to protect children's health.

Since plants contain more carbohydrate matter than oils, biodiesel production uses up to five times more land than ethanol production. This limits the potential contribution of biodiesel to the energy supply. However, biodiesel can also be made from waste oils and animal fats. A year's worth of Europe's waste cooking oil could be turned into over 260 million gallons (1 billion liters) of biodiesel.

CASE STUDY: A Spanish biodiesel project

In the Ribera district of Spain, waste oil from restaurants, fast-food chains, and the food manufacturing industry in 32 towns is collected, processed into biodiesel, and dispensed from the local gasoline stations. The project was originally set up to fuel public transportation and government vehicles, but all citizens can now buy biofuel to use in their cars. Over 400 restaurants participate in the scheme. The Ribera Energy Agency (Agència Energètica de la Ribera) is now piloting tanks in markets and city halls to collect waste cooking oil from individual households. Safety is a key concern, since cooking oil catches fire easily.

THE ARGUMENT: Biodiesel is a good fuel for vehicles

For:
- It releases less carbon monoxide and sulphur than diesel.
- It can be distributed within current infrastructure.
- It can be used in existing engines.
- It contains no lead additives.
- It biodegrades more easily than oil-based fuels.
- It is a convenient source of energy in isolated rural areas.
- It is good for new engines.
- It is safer to store and transport than oil.
- It can power heavy machinery and vehicles.
- Diesel engines are more efficient than gasoline engines.

Against:
- Production is relatively expensive.
- Biodiesel production uses more land than ethanol production.
- Cost reduction potential is low.
- It emits more nitrogen oxides than regular diesel.
- It is problematic in cold temperatures.
- It can damage older engines.

Using organic waste on a large scale

Burning waste for energy, or breaking it down in biogas digesters, is used widely in LEDCs. Many countries also use household and agricultural waste to produce heat or electricity on a large scale.

Waste from sugar

Sugar cane waste, for example, is an important source of industrial energy in Cuba, Brazil, India, and Zimbabwe. Farming in Denmark generates large amounts of waste straw. Around 1.3 million tons of straw a year are bought by power companies and used to generate electricity.

△ The products of landfill sites can be burned to release energy, or decomposed under controlled conditions to produce a type of biogas called biomethane.

Municipal solid waste

MEDCs, such as Austria, France, the U.K., Finland, and the U.S., have established power stations that burn landfill products. All waste incinerators in Switzerland have to be modified, so that the heat released from burning rubbish can be used to generate electricity, and about 40 percent of French household waste is burned to produce electricity or heat for urban heating systems. Uppsala, a city in Sweden, burns household rubbish to provide 42 percent of the heating energy required for the district.

Biomethane

A biogas digester heats up and breaks down biomass to make biomethane. In Sweden, methane generated from agricultural waste, manure, and grassy crops is used to generate electricity, heat homes, and fuel vehicles. Biomethane gas powers more than 8,000 buses, rubbish trucks, and passenger cars. Currently, 65 Swedish filling stations sell biomethane.

Biomethane is developed from sources that would normally release methane into the atmosphere, causing global warming. Burning methane converts it into CO_2, which is less harmful to the environment. Just like natural gas, biomethane can be distributed through pipelines and is sometimes used to "top up" natural gas supplies.

Human waste can also be used in biogas digesters. A Swedish housing project in Stockholm has a special waste collection system. All biowaste, including sewage, is fed to a biogas generator that produces gas and electricity for the city. The waste from a single household produces enough biogas to service the household's gas cooker. Heat generated by the digester is used to warm the apartments.

THE ARGUMENT: Biogas digesters are a good source of energy in rural areas

For:
- Biogas digesters are a reliable and clean energy source.
- They remove the smell from slurry.
- They reduce water pollution by using up waste that would end up in rivers.
- They preserve the nutrients in manure, which can be used for fertilizer.
- They are a convenient, local source of energy.
- They can be used anywhere.
- They prevent the release of methane.
- They produce a sludge that can be used as animal feed or fertilizer.
- They are hygienic—directly using animal dung on fields can spread disease.

Against:
- Digesters must stay at 95°F (35°C), so need energy in cold weather.
- They are expensive—even a small digester can cost $900. They also need to be built well to avoid leaks.
- Drought or food shortages that affect animals would disrupt both food and energy supply.

CHAPTER 4

The environment and resources

Biomass is a controversial energy source. In LEDCs around the world, burning biomass for heating and cooking is causing serious air pollution. Much current biomass use is not only dangerous, but it is also unsustainable.

Around 55 percent of the world's forests are in LEDCs, and only about 3 percent are plantations. Millions of acres of forest are lost each year through overcollection of fuelwood to meet the needs of growing populations. In LEDCs, billions are being invested in developing liquid and solid biofuels, but critics argue that biomass will never be clean or renewable.

Is biomass really carbon neutral?

As we saw earlier, the amount of carbon given off by burning biomass cannot be more than the plant took in when it was growing. Supporters argue that providing biomass sources are replanted, no extra CO_2 will be added to the Earth's atmosphere. However, this does not take into account the energy used to make fertilizers and pesticides, farm and harvest the crop, transport the biomass to a power plant, and process it into usable fuel. Yet more energy is used in building processing plants and distribution networks. At the moment, most of this energy input comes from fossil fuels, which emit greenhouse gases.

The production of ethanol from corn crops in the U.S. is very controversial. Corn is expensive to grow and uses large amounts of water and energy— some scientists say up to 29 percent more energy than it returns as fuel. But in 2004, the U.S. Department of Agriculture reported that corn ethanol production returns 67 percent more energy than it uses. New developments will help to reduce the impact of ethanol production. One solution is to burn agricultural waste to generate the power that runs the plants.

Energy crops

Future energy crops must be chosen carefully. The ideal crop would grow rapidly, and use few chemicals and limited water to minimize energy input. At the moment, straw and willow crops have the lowest carbon emissions per unit of energy delivered. *Perennial crops* (those crops that can be harvested without uprooting them) are more environmentally friendly than row crops such as corn, which need to be replanted every year.

> **Ethanol is not helping us. It's encouraging the importation of oil from Saudi Arabia and elsewhere [because it uses fossil fuels in its production].**
>
> David Pimentel, professor of ecology and agriculture, Cornell University

Furthermore, perennial crops planted on poor land can actually improve soil quality, prevent wind and water erosion, and provide new habitats. They also require less nitrogen-based fertilizers, which are responsible for up to 80 percent of nitrogen oxide emissions (another greenhouse gas known to be 269 times more damaging to the environment than CO_2). In 2000, a United Nations Environment Programme (UNEP) report suggested that disruption to the nitrogen cycle may be damaging our environment as much as the disruption to the carbon cycle.

A carbon trap

Unlike other sources, biomass can actually absorb CO_2 released by burning fossil fuels. Some crops live for up to ten years storing carbon. Scientists say that 20 percent of CO_2 released yearly by fossil fuels could be absorbed by planting energy crops.

▽ The carbon cycle illustrates the "carbon neutral" theory. Biomass fuels can be carbon neutral if they are produced in a responsible and sustainable way.

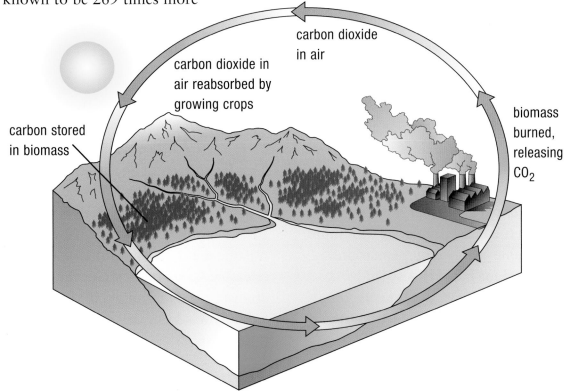

carbon dioxide in air

carbon dioxide in air reabsorbed by growing crops

carbon stored in biomass

biomass burned, releasing CO_2

Is it really sustainable?

The world's forests are sources of fuelwood, animal fodder, medicines, fruits, and construction materials. Agroforestry (farming trees) and natural forest management methods also promise to make wood an efficient energy crop. An average of 3 tons of dry wood per acre per year can be harvested in a sustainable way from forests. As with biomass, it produces 22 times more energy than is used to grow and harvest it. It has been calculated that around 100 million acres of woody biomass could supply the United States with about 1.5 billion kilowatt-hours of energy by the year 2050.

Forest protection

However, some environmental groups are against the use of wood as biomass. In Australia, the classification of forestry by-products (such as woodchips) as renewable energy sources is highly controversial. Some people believe it will encourage forest clearance by making the timber industry more profitable.

Energy plantations

Another danger is that huge areas of forest could be replaced with more profitable energy crop plantations. Demand for biofuels is rising by 25 percent a year. In Germany, for example, biodiesel production has

doubled since 2003, and there are plans to burn palm oil in power stations. It is cheaper for European producers to buy palm oil from LEDCs, than it is to use home-grown rapeseed oil. As a result, many ancient rain forests in Southeast Asia are being cut down to plant profitable palm oil plantations.

" The expansion of palm oil production is one of the leading causes of rain forest destruction in Southeast Asia. It is one of the most environmentally damaging commodities on the planet. Once again, we are trying to solve our problems by dumping them in developing countries, where they have devastating effects on local people. "

Simon Counsell, director of Rainforest Foundation, U.K.

The destruction of ancient forests brings many problems. The dead organic matter in forest soils is a large store of carbon. In energy plantations, organic matter rots much faster, releasing CO_2 and methane into the atmosphere. Natural plant and animal habitats would be destroyed, leading to a loss of biodiversity. Disease, pests, and natural disasters could easily destroy large plantations of single energy crops, known as *monocultures*. This would lead to the extensive use of pesticides and insecticides—chemicals that would damage the environment further. Environmental groups such as World Wildlife Fund and Friends of the Earth are calling for eco-certification to make sure biofuel promotion does not do more harm to the environment than good.

▽ Palm oil plantations in Malaysia cover almost an eighth of the country. The fruit of the trees is rich in oils, and is used to make biodiesel.

Reforestation

Many MEDCs have seen the threats of deforestation and are carefully managing their own forests. Countries, such as Germany and France, offer subsidies for reforestation, and encourage companies to compensate for fossil fuel use by planting trees to absorb CO_2. U.K. forest cover has increased due to incentives for tree planting. New forests are important carbon traps for offsetting emissions now, and key sources of renewable biomass energy in the future. Another advantage is that forestry by-products are more useful than those of crops such as rapeseed or sugar cane.

Health risks and benefits

Toxic substances present in exhaust gases can have a serious impact on health, especially tiny particles that settle deep into the lungs, causing diseases, such as cancer. Burning biomass fuels releases fewer polluting emissions than burning fossil fuels. This makes them attractive potential alternatives to gasoline and diesel. However, most current biomass use is actually causing serious health problems in the world's LEDCs. Biomass will only be classed as "clean" fuel if the right technology is used.

Air pollution

Traditional biomass fuels are widely used for cooking and heating in Africa, Southeast Asia, and parts of Latin America. Burning wood over open fires releases more than 200 different chemicals, including 14 that can cause cancer. This is having a serious impact on the health of populations. The World Health Organisation (WHO) reports that 1.6 million people die every year due to indoor air pollution.

Wood smoke contains pollutants, such as carbon monoxide and nitrogen oxides. Long-term exposure to wood smoke can cause respiratory infections, lung disease, cancer and eye irritation. Even in the United States, where clean technology is available, wood smoke

causes illnesses that kill around 30,000 people a year. Collecting fuelwood is also hard work and time consuming. Women and children in rural areas spend more than two hours a day collecting and carrying wood, animal feed, and grass. This limits the chance for development through childcare, education, and activities that make money for the family. The demand for wood has also worsened deforestation in some areas, creating a "fuelwood crisis."

▽ The waste parts of many crops are already burned as biofuel in many LEDCs, such as here in northern Nigeria.

Acid rain

Fossil fuels contain a high proportion of sulphur, released as sulphur dioxide when they are burned. Biomass contains around 40 times less sulphur than even the cleanest coal, but the sulphur dioxide it releases contributes to acid rain. In power plants that burn biomass, filters and chemicals can be used to trap pollutants.

Energy from waste

Today, most household waste goes in landfill sites or is incinerated. Rotting waste releases potent methane into the air. The amount of methane in the atmosphere has increased by 150 percent since 1750. Collecting methane as a source of biomass energy could help to tackle this increase. An Australian company uses waste food, liquid, and paper to feed a biogas digester at Camellia, Sydney. The biogas is used to generate electricity and heat. In the U.S., 400 landfill sites can collect and use biogas. In 2004, these units produced around 9 billion kilowatt-hours of electricity—just 0.2 percent of U.S. electricity production.

Waste can also be burned directly to release heat energy, disposing of waste much quicker than landfill sites. But this can release toxic chemicals into the air. These should be removed and treated with a nonburn technology, before the waste or methane is burned. The final danger is that using waste for energy will encourage people to put less effort into recycling.

CASE STUDY:
Sewage to fuel in Lille, France

In Lille, France, over 4 million car and bus journeys are made every day. To reduce polluting emissions, the city uses biogas as a fuel for more than 500 buses. The project began in the 1990s, with biogas collected from sewage plants. The gas given off by rotting sewage contains a lot of methane. It is collected, cleaned, and used alongside natural gas in engines that perform as well as conventional diesel buses. Heavy gas tanks add an extra weight to each bus, reducing the distance that can be traveled on each tank of fuel to 93 miles (150 kilometers), but the buses are much less noisy and smelly. Compared to diesel fuel, biogas produces lower nitrogen oxide and particle emissions, and is much safer to store, because it is not so flammable. A new biogas power plant in Lille will produce enough biogas from household waste to fuel 100 extra buses.

Land use and location issues

A key advantage of biomass energy is that it can be obtained from an enormous range of sources. The technology can be adapted to suit local crops, so it can be developed in almost every country in the world. The only limitation is the growth rates of plants and the amount of farmland available to use. A study carried out by the University of Florida calculated that replacing the entire United States' fuel supply with corn ethanol would use at least 60 percent of cropland in the U.S.

▽ Biomass is bulky and expensive to transport. It is better to build power plants close to crops.

Some scientists believe that using land to grow fuel crops will increase the problem of food shortages in the LEDCs of the world. However, many countries in the world have food surpluses, and large areas of land are currently used to grow "luxury" items, such as pet foods, coffee, and tobacco. Tackling the issues of hunger will require political action, more than additional land.

Sustainable forestry could potentially produce biofuels while protecting the environment and food production. Biomass crops could also be grown on wastelands such as disused mining sites or land that is out of production.

In the United Kingdom alone, over a million acres of land are currently "set aside," which means that farmers are paid to do nothing with the land to avoid the overproduction of food supplies in the country. Utilizing 80 percent of this unused land to grow energy crops would provide enough biofuel to make up 2 percent of all gasoline sold in the U.K.

> " Land will be pressed into use, not just to produce energy, but to replace the raw materials for much of our industry that are currently based on petroleum. "
>
> Ben Gill, U.K. government's biomass taskforce

Using crop waste

Another potential source of bioenergy is the waste from existing crops. The technology to use these efficiently is under development (see page 41). However, some people are worried that this will have a negative effect on soil quality. At the moment, most crop residues are returned to the soil, where they rot to form humus. This helps to replace soil nutrients, helps keep air and water in the soil, and reduces erosion.

The ash left when biomass is burned can be returned to the soil, but it contains only a small percentage of the nutrients applied to the soil as fertilizer. It would be better to take a certain fraction of the crop residues for energy and return the rest to the soil. This would be more sustainable and could still meet a significant proportion of energy needs.

THE ARGUMENT:
Land should be used to grow energy crops

For:
- A large proportion of farmland in MEDCs is currently unused.
- There is actually a net food surplus in the world.
- Energy crops can be planted on land that is not suitable for growing food crops.

Against:
- Food crops in LEDCs might be replaced with more profitable energy crops.
- Burning all parts of a crop means that no plant nutrients are returned to the soil.

◁ This man is harvesting cacao nuts in Ghana. Cacao nuts can produce up to 63 gallons (240 liters) of biodiesel per 2.5 acres (1 hectare).

In Ghana, for example, biodiesel fuel is produced from fast-growing nuts. This is likely to save Ghana $238 million on oil imports.

Farming communities would also benefit from a new market for their crops and crop residues. In 2007, a plant in Norfolk, England, will begin the production of bioethanol from locally grown sugar beet. Around 700,000 tons of sugar beet crops will be used to produce up to 18 million gallons (70 million liters) of bioethanol a year.

" If the hundreds of billions of dollars that now flow into [the oil industry] in a few nations were to flow instead to the millions of people who till the world's fields [to grow biofuel crops], most countries would see substantial national security, economic, and environmental benefits. **"**

Senator Richard Lugar and R. James Woolsey, The New Petroleum, 1999

A local industry

Compared with fossil fuels, biomass fuels are bulky and expensive to transport. However, unlike fossil fuels, different forms of biomass are found all over the world. If processing plants were built close to the biomass supply, this would reduce transportation costs as well as the amount of energy that a country would need to import.

However, relying on a supply of local crops limits the scale of bioenergy production. Japan, for example, is one of the world's largest energy users, but has little agricultural land. Locally grown biomass is not a sustainable option. Biofuels must be produced on a huge scale to be economically viable. The carbon savings from Norfolk in England's bioethanol production will be equivalent to taking 50,000 cars off the road. However, 1,300 times as many cars are added to the world's roads every year.

To meet the target of including 5.75 percent biofuels in European fuels by 2010, energy crops would have to be planted on almost 2 percent of European farmland. This is possible, but it is not cost effective because European farmers expect higher payment for their crops than farmers in LEDCs. The European Union (EU) will rely on cheaper fuel imports from countries such as Brazil, which exported around 0.7 billion gallons (2.6 billion liters) of ethanol in 2005.

Careful planning is needed to establish a fair international market for energy crops. There is a danger that they could replicate patterns of food production, whereby some countries produce an enormous surplus, and import cheap crops from nations that struggle to feed their own people.

In the U.S., control of the ethanol production process is already moving away from individual farmers, to large corporations, meaning that the profits will not benefit the farmers directly.

Not on my doorstep
Although most people like the idea of renewable energy, they are less happy about having technology, such as waste incinerators, genetically modified crops, and biomass power plants, built near their homes. This can be a big obstacle to clean energy planners.

CASE STUDY: Protesting against renewable energy

In April 2006, plans to build Europe's biggest biomass power station in Devon, England, were rejected. The Winkleigh gasifier plant would have converted local energy crops, forest residues, clean wood waste, and compost into fuel that would be able to fire a gas turbine, generating 23 megawatts of electricity—enough to power 23,000 local homes. Hundreds of people objected, saying the project was too large for the 9-acre (3.6-hectare) site, and that transporting the biomass to the power station would disrupt the local countryside.

Cost and investment

Unlike solar, wave, and water power, almost every country in the world has the potential to use local biomass for energy. However, the contribution of biomass energy to total consumption varies widely around the world.

In Finland, more than 12 percent of electricity is generated from bioenergy. In the U.S., this figure is just 1.7 percent. The uptake of biomass energy will rely on government support to raise demand and encourage the development of clean technology.

Tax incentives and subsidies

One way that governments can raise demand is by subsidizing the cost of producing and buying bioenergy. Ethanol production from corn is heavily subsidized in the United States. The national government will provide a subsidy of 14 cents per gallon until 2010, and five states (Hawaii, Minnesota, Missouri, Montana, and Washington) currently insist on 10 percent ethanol in all gasoline sold. This has helped corn ethanol to become the most widespread alternative fuel, despite warnings from many energy scientists that in the long run, it is not energy efficient or economical,

it does not improve energy security, and it does not ensure clean air. In 2006, a total of $2.8 billion was invested in ethanol production.

One reason behind U.S. support for ethanol as a fuel of the future is that it can be easily blended with gasoline to make "gasohol." The technology to make it is available, and existing car engines can run on gasohol blends. In contrast, hydrogen—another potential fuel of the future—would need new engine designs and filling stations. The U.S. Energy Policy Act (EPACT) of 2005 requires 7,400 million gallons (28,000 million liters) of ethanol and biodiesel to enter the fuel supply by 2012. This will power almost 6 percent of vehicles used in the United States.

The International Energy Agency (IEA) predicts that world consumption of ethanol will triple by 2020. In some parts of the world, the price of biofuels is already falling below that of gasoline and diesel, and this is driving demand. In Brazil, ethanol is less than half the price of gas. The French government taxes fuel blenders that do not incorporate biofuels. In 2006, Germany introduced a tax on biofuels, since tax subsidies are no longer needed to drive demand.

CASE STUDY:
China's sweet solution

China is the world's second largest energy user after the United States. By 2020, the IEA predicts that China's greenhouse gas emissions will have more than doubled. The Chinese government is anxious to reduce its dependency on coal, oil, and polluting biomass fuels, such as wood and dung, used in rural areas. In 2005, it pledged to switch 15 percent of China's energy consumption to renewable sources and has committed over $168 billion over 15 years to research and development. By studying Brazil's methods, China has become the world's third largest ethanol producer. Since corn is an important food source in China, alternative starchy plants, such as cassava, sugar cane, and sweet potatoes, are being developed as ethanol crops.

Growing corporate investment

The United States and the European Union are aiming to meet almost 6 percent of transportation fuel needs with biofuels within the next six years. These fixed targets give the bioenergy industry a guarantee that its technology will be in demand, and will encourage investment in renewable power. The green energy consultancy, Clean Edge, predicts that the world's market for biofuels is likely to reach $50.6 billion by 2015. However, there is still a long way to go to match the hundreds of billions of dollars that are earned by the oil industry each year.

Some of the biggest investors are oil companies, who are being encouraged to use their huge wealth to develop solutions to the energy crisis. For example, the Shell oil company invested over $938 million in renewable energies and is the largest blender of biofuels. However, this investment is still a tiny fraction of the money spent exploring for oil each year.

▽ The Choren-Alpha power plant in Germany was the first to produce fuel from woodchips.

CASE STUDY:
Oil company investment in biofuels

In 2006, the BP oil company pledged to spend $535 million over the next ten years on setting up an energy laboratory to explore alternative fuels, including biofuels. The first research programs started in 2007, focusing on developing new biofuels such as butanol; improving the efficiency of the fuels ethanol and biodiesel; finding ways to convert a greater proportion of crops into fuel; and developing plants that produce more "energy molecules" (such as starches and oils) that will grow on land not suitable for food crops. The company also begun to sell "E85," a blend of 85 percent ethanol and 15 percent gasoline, in the U.S. in 2006. Biobutanol was introduced into U.K. gasoline in 2007.

Most governments also support their fossil fuel industries more than they support renewable energies. For example, the United States government subsidizes the production of gasoline, making it cheaper than bottled water. If carbon emissions and fossil fuel use were heavily taxed, people would switch to renewables much more quickly. However, green policies like this are very unpopular with industry and voters. Policies to encourage bioenergy also face heavy opposition from the petrochemical, forest products, waste, and recycling industries.

> You look at the promise that ethanol gives us... Do you do it with tax credits, do you do it with incentives, do you do it with subsidies? But we sure as heck want to jump-start it.

Rudy Giuliani, potential U.S. presidential candidate, speaking in support of ethanol subsidies in Iowa, in May 2006

However, it seems that energy policies are moving to the top of the agenda. The technology to use bioenergy on a large scale will spread faster if people are willing to share their knowledge. In June 2006, Sweden and California agreed to work together to develop biofuels for transportation and other uses. Sweden is a leader in biomethane production, and California is anxious to develop its own biogas program.

△ Demand for oil-based transportation fuel is expected to rise by 1.4 percent every year until 2030. Biofuels may help to meet some of this demand.

Energy efficiency

The most important action that governments can take is to encourage people to become more efficient energy users. Many politicians and industry leaders believe that protecting the climate will damage our standard of living by increasing the cost of energy—and everything that uses it. *Energy efficiency* actually means making each unit of energy work harder for us. This reduces energy bills, reduces greenhouse gas emissions and makes renewable technologies more realistic energy alternatives. The land area needed to grow energy crops for biofuel, for example, would be less if cars used fuel more efficiently.

> ❝ We ought to be purchasing energy efficiency to save money. If we do it right, the environmental benefit comes free. ❞
>
> Amory Lovins, consultant physicist and chief executive officer, Rocky Mountain Institute

Vehicle efficiency

Our transportation systems consume almost 60 percent of the world's oil. This is one of the most difficult parts of the climate problem to deal with, because millions of new cars are joining the world's roads every year. Cars are highly inefficient machines, with just 13 percent of the energy available in fuel reaching the wheels. The rest of the energy is wasted as heat and noise, or is used to power accessories, such as air conditioning.

Smaller, lighter, slower cars are more efficient, because they travel farther on the same amount of fuel. Fuel savings can be attractive to customers, but most people prefer their cars to be comfortable, safe, and fast, rather than kind to the environment. One option may be to build big cars with lightweight materials, more efficient engines and aerodynamic design, all of which will reduce fuel consumption.

To introduce measures, such as taxing large, inefficient vehicles and lowering speed limits on the roads, would be effective, but policies like this are very unpopular with the public. Governments also need to look at ways of reducing the number of car journeys that people make. Sprawling, suburban housing developments, out-of-town shopping malls, and expensive, unreliable public transportation systems all encourage people to use their cars more.

CASE STUDY:
Combined heat and power in Sweden

Växjö, a city in Sweden, is aiming to become a "fossil fuel-free" city. A combined heat and power plant in the city burns 100 percent biomass fuels, such as woodchips, bark, and peat, generating around 37 megawatts of electricity. Combined heat and power plants distribute the heat generated by electricity production around nearby homes, rather than letting it go to waste in cooling towers.

This makes the power plant twice as efficient—since twice as much of the fuel energy becomes useful energy. The thermal energy generated in Växjö is used to heat water for most of the city's housing estates and nearby industries. When the price of electricity is low, the power plant produces more heat and less electricity. CO_2 emissions from heating in the city have decreased by 69 percent in seven years.

CHAPTER 6

Biomass power in the future

Biomass energy is seen as one of the most promising renewable energy sources. If it is used in a clean and sustainable way, it could benefit the environment, local communities, and provide countries with a source of energy that does not depend on imports. Some existing bioenergy technologies, such as corn ethanol, may not be sustainable in the long term, but they are encouraging investment in technologies that could be used on a large scale in the future.

Biodiesel from biomass

One of the most promising developments is the technology to convert waste plant matter into biofuels. This would greatly reduce the demand for extra land. At the moment, cost-effective biofuels can be made only by using energy crops. Agricultural waste by-products, such as woodchips, contain a significant amount of cellulose that cannot be fermented or pressed into oils.

This type of biomass can be turned into gas by thermochemical means, and the gas can be converted into liquid fuel, but the extra stage is

> **"**Advanced biofuels will be based on biomass residues, which will increase the yield, decrease the cost, and decouple their production from that of food.**"**
>
> Jean Cadu, strategic fuels development manager, Shell Bio-fuels

expensive. However, a new type of biodiesel fuel that has been developed in Germany uses thermal processing techniques to turn solid biomass directly into a liquid ready for

▽ Didcot power station in England cofires a range of biomass materials along with coal.

processing into fuel. This combination of biochemical and thermochemical processing has great potential as a source of cost-effective and energy-efficient biofuel of the future. The cost involved is higher than regular biodiesel, but prices will fall as demand for clean fuel rises and it is produced on a large scale.

Shell oil company plans to build the world's largest biomass-to-liquid refinery in Germany, with the aim to produce 16,500 tons of fuel a year.

Ethanol from biomass

Ethanol could also be produced from agricultural waste. Straw is cheap but high in cellulose. Specially designed enzymes can break down straw into sugars for fermenting. This technology could be applied to other types of agricultural waste. More than a third of U.S. gasoline consumption could be made from agricultural waste each year. The National Resources Defense Council have predicted that using cellulosic sources, ethanol could replace all gasoline use by 2050.

CASE STUDY:
Electricity from weeds

A pilot project in Australia is using a weed called *mimosa* to generate electricity. Mimosa spreads quickly and grows densely, often replacing all indigenous plants in an area. The thorny weed grows in large quantities on the Adelaide river floodplain, and when it is cut back, it regenerates itself after 3 to 5 years. This makes it an ideal source of cellulosic biomass energy.

Thermochemical processing is used to turn the harvested mimosa into fuel gas that can run an electricity generator. The gas is rich in hydrogen, so it could also potentially be used in fuel cells.

The pilot scheme should produce enough electricity to power about 200 homes in the city of Darwin, reducing greenhouse gas emissions by over 2,600 tons of CO_2 every year. The cost of the power that is produced is currently around 24 cents per kilowatt-hour, but costs would fall if the scheme were scaled up. The mimosa weeds must be harvested carefully to avoid spreading its seeds, which would compete with nearby food crops and wild plants. Using mimosa as a renewable energy source would raise funds to keep it under control, and to keep it from spreading through the Northern Australian wetlands.

"Designer" energy crops

Genetic engineering is being used to design energy crops that grow faster and consume more CO_2. These crops have been nicknamed "smog-eaters." By using smog-eaters, the production of biofuels could be made more efficient. For example, corn that does not need fertilizer would use a great deal less energy in its production. The microbes used during ethanol fermentation are also being genetically modified to speed up production. However, genetic modification is controversial. Pests or disease could easily wipe out large, genetically identical monocultures. Since energy crops are not eaten, modifying them may be more acceptable to the public.

Methanol

Thermal processing can convert wood and other biomass into methanol, which can be used directly as a fuel or converted to gasoline. The only by-product is wood ash, which can be used as a fertilizer. The technology is in the early stages of development, but it could become an important energy resource in the future. By using wood and forest residues, the process can be more than 50 percent efficient. However, large areas of sustainable forests would be needed. A pilot plant in Japan has produced methanol from ricebran and sawdust and, in Europe, industrial paper waste is being used. Methanol can also be produced from biogas, which can be made from manure in a biogas digester. In Utah, there are plans afoot to produce 8,000 gallons (30,000 liters) of methanol a day from the manure of 250,000 pigs.

THE ARGUMENT:
We should experiment with genetically modified energy crops

For:
- Crops can be modified to grow faster using less fertilizer and land.
- Modified, pest-resistant crops need fewer pesticides.
- Crops would be cheaper to grow, producing cheaper fuel.
- Crops may offer largest potential benefit to LEDCs.

Against:
- There may be unexpected consequences of "playing with nature."
- Modified crops could become "superweeds," competing with existing plants for light and water.
- Modified plants may cause new, serious allergies in humans.
- Pests would evolve to become insecticide-resistant.
- Large areas of genetically identical plants would affect biodiversity.

Hydrogen from biomass

Hydrogen is a nonpolluting fuel that can be used in a fuel cell to power cars. Some people believe it is the fuel of the future. Currently, producing hydrogen uses much more energy than the hydrogen gives back. However, researchers are finding ways to make the gas using renewable energies—including biomass. Bacteria produce small amounts of hydrogen when they break down human waste water. Scientists can quadruple production by passing an electric current through the water. In the future, hydrogen fuel could be collected as sewage is cleaned.

Biomass from water

Oceans, lakes, rivers, and wetlands cover over 70 percent of the planet. They could produce an enormous source of biomass energy without using agricultural land, because they contain algae. Most of the world's oil resources were formed from algae that died millions of years ago. Algae can be grown quickly in large ponds or in areas of ocean, and pressed to extract oil. Some scientists predict that 43,000 square feet (4,000 square meters) of algae could produce over 3,500 gallons (13,000 liters) of biodiesel a year.

Japanese energy scientists are currently interested in the idea of growing large quantities of seaweed, with the aim of turning it into methanol or fermenting it to produce biogas. However, like all energy alternatives, these projects need huge investment in production facilities.

▽ Some species of algae contain 50 percent natural oils—a potential source of biodiesel.

Developing biomass energy

Rising energy bills, climate concern, fears about energy security, and improved technology are all increasing the demand for renewable power. Many types of biomass energy are being explored. Biomass can be converted into solid, liquid, and gas fuels, to power everything from vehicles to electricity generators. Sources grow all around the world and can be used at both a local and large scale. However, the first challenge is choosing which type of bioenergy to invest in.

Most current use of biomass energy is neither clean nor sustainable. The pollution caused by burning wood, manure, and agricultural waste in LEDCs is causing severe health problems. Some energy crops have a bigger energy and environmental cost than they return. If biomass is to be a vital part of the future energy mix, we need to find ways to process and use it in a sustainable way. As LEDCs continue to develop, their energy needs will increase. There is a shared responsibility to try and meet this demand in sustainable ways. Wealthier countries can help LEDCs by sharing knowledge and helping to fund such developments. Corporations must also be encouraged to share the technology needed to generate and use biomass energy in a sustainable way.

"Energy mix"

Biofuels and bioenergy will not be the only answer to our energy problems, but are an important part of the move from dependency on fossil fuels to an "energy mix" of renewable resources.

> " Agriculture in the twenty-first century will become our oil wells. "
>
> Larry Russo, U.S. Department of Energy, Office of the Biomass Program

There are already promising projects that combine biomass energy with solar and wind power. Superefficient biogas digesters heated by solar power, and biomass-fueled generators to back up wind turbines are good examples. It is key that investment continues at local and national levels. Programmes that provide improved biomass stoves to millions of households in LEDCs are just as important as research into ambitious new technologies, such as harvesting algae.

Becoming "energy wise"

As we develop alternative energies, our priority as individuals, communities, and industries should be to use our existing supply more efficiently.

This is the easiest way to tackle carbon emissions. It will also make alternative energies, such as biofuels, more viable in the long term. Preventable energy waste costs the world more than $938 billion every year. About 5 percent of U.S. and 7 percent of U.K. domestic electricity use is lost to appliances left in standby mode. Many cheap energy-efficient products are available, but people either do not know about them, or they do not know how important it is to use them.

So far, little has been done to boost energy efficiency. In many countries, taxpayer-funded subsidies have made energy seem cheap. Bad habits, such as leaving cellphone chargers plugged in, televisions on standby, and using cars for short trips, are hard to change. Therefore, governments have a responsibility to educate the public about the environmental and economic benefits of using less energy. Countries also need to share with each other the technology needed to use energy efficiently. Energy savings would help to speed up development, by saving money that can be used to fight disease and educate populations.

▷ A huge global effort is needed to curb energy consumption and develop efficient technologies and alternative energy sources for the future.

Biodiesel Liquid fuel made from oily plants, such as soybeans and rapeseed.

Bioenergy The energy produced from biomass.

Bioethanol Liquid alcohol fuel made from starchy plants, such as corn.

Biofuel The fuel made from biomass.

Biogas Gas fuel produced when organic matter is broken down by microbes.

Biomethane Methane produced by rotting biomass.

Butanol A colorless alcohol that can be mixed with gasoline and used as fuel.

By-products The substances produced by a process that is carried out for a different purpose.

Carbohydrate An organic compound made from carbon, hydrogen, and oxygen.

Catalyst A substance that activates or speeds up a chemical reaction without reacting itself.

Cellulose The main substance that makes up the cell walls of plants.

Coppice Cutting back trees to encourage rapid growth.

Fermented When something is broken down into simpler substances by a microorganism, such as the breaking down of sugar into ethanol by yeast.

Fossil fuels Coal, oil, and gas formed over millions of years from the remains of plants and animals.

Fuel cell A device that converts chemical energy in a fuel directly to electric energy without burning.

Fuelwood Wood collected for heating, cooking, and lighting.

Gasification Converting organic matter directly to gas using high temperatures and chemical processes.

Gasifier A device in which gasification takes place.

Gasohol A gasoline and ethanol blend.

Greenhouse effect The warming of the Earth's climate due to gases in the atmosphere that trap solar heat before it can be radiated back into space.

Perennial Plants that live for more than two growing seasons. Perennials can be harvested several times.

Scrubber Chemicals or devices that can remove certain impurities from a gas.

Sustainable Something that can be maintained without depleting a natural resource.

Thermochemical A process that uses both heat and chemical methods.

Yield The amount of a crop that is produced.

Books to read

Energy Sources: Biomass Power Neil Morris; Watts, London, 2006: a detailed look at biomass power and the economic, social, and environmental concerns around it.

Sustainable World: Energy Rob Bowden; Wayland, London, 2003: looks at how to use energy for a sustainable future.

Energy Forever?: Geothermal and Bio-energy Ian Graham; Wayland, London, 2001: discusses the issues around geothermal and bioenergy.

Alternative Energy Christine Petersen; Children's Press, Danbury, 2004: a detailed look at the different types of alternative energy and their place in society.

Web Sites

Due to the changing nature of Internet links, The Rosen Publishing Group, Inc., has developed an online list of Web sites related to the subject of this book. This site is updated regularly. Please use this link to access the list:
www.rosenlinks.com/ted/bio/

Index

Note: Page numbers in *italic* refer to illustrations.